Collective Biographies

CONGRESSIONAL MEDAL OF HONOR RECIPIENTS

Kieran Doherty

Enslow Publishers, Inc.

44 Fadem Road   PO Box 38
Box 699   Aldershot
Springfield, NJ 07081   Hants GU12 6BP
USA   UK

To Lynne, my wife and helper.

Library of Congress Cataloging-in-Publication Data

Doherty, Kieran.
  Congressional Medal of Honor recipients / Kieran Doherty.
    p. cm.
  Includes bibliographical references (p.) and index.
  Summary: Biographies of eleven recipients of America's highest military honor:
Jacob Parrott, William Carney, Mary Edwards Walker, Eddie Rickenbacker, Alvin
York, John Bulkeley, Mitchell Red Cloud, Hiroshi Miyamura, Jay Vargas, Gary
Gordon, and Randall Shughart.
    ISBN 0-7660-1026-0
    1. Medal of Honor—Juvenile literature. 2. United States—Armed Forces—
Biography—Juvenile literature. [1. United States—Armed Forces—Biography.
2. Medal of Honor. 3. Afro-Americans—Biography. 4. Japanese Americans—
Biography.] I. title.
UB433.D64 1998
355.1'342—dc21
  [B]   97-23056
                                                           CIP
                                                            AC

Printed in the United States of America

10 9 8 7 6 5 4 3 2 1

Illustration Credits: Andy Porter, Photographer, Gallup, New Mexico, pp.
74, 82; Congressional Medal of Honor Society, pp. 8, 26, 36, 54, 64, 84, 94,
100; Courtesy of the Prints and Photographs Division, Library of Congress,
pp. 72, 81; Ho Chunk Historic Preservation Department, p. 69; Library of
Congress, pp. 16, 23; Massachusetts Commandery Military Order of the
Loyal Legion and the US Army Military History Institute, p. 18; National
Archives, pp. 14, 28, 41, 43, 46, 52, 59, 62, 88; Oswego County Historical
Society, Oswego, New York, p. 34; Sirlin Photographers, Sacramento, CA,
p. 92.

Cover Illustration: National Archives.

Contents

Acknowledgments

The author wishes to express sincere thanks to the staff of the Lake Worth City Library: the staff of the Palm Beach Community College Central Campus Library; the Medal of Honor Society; the Oswego, N.Y. Historical Society and the Ho-Chunk Indian Nation.

Introduction

America has often found it necessary to wage war. Throughout its history, American men and women have fought and died for their country on battlefields around the world. Thousands of these men and women were unsung heroes and heroines in battles from Concord, Massachusetts, to Mogadishu, Somalia. A handful of these have been awarded the Medal of Honor for bravery in combat above and beyond the call of duty.

Until the time of the Civil War, there was no such thing as the Medal of Honor. (Though most people call the medal the Congressional Medal of Honor, its proper name is simply the Medal of Honor.) In December of 1861, the Congress of the United States decided some special award was needed for those who displayed special bravery. The first Medals of Honor were awarded in 1863 to recognize a band of Union Army raiders who struck a blow at the heart of the Confederacy. The most recent recipients were two soldiers who were killed in action in Somalia in 1993. A total of 3,427 medals have been presented. Most of those—2,362—have been awarded to Army men. Nineteen men are so-called double recipients. That means they were awarded two medals for different actions under fire.

Those who have been awarded medals have been as diverse as America itself. They were rich and poor; African American, Asian American, Native American, Hispanic American, and white American; young and old; from big cities and country villages. Some were the sons of families that had been in America for generations. Others were immigrants who came to America to find a better life. Even though women have traditionally been kept out of combat, one woman, Dr. Mary Edwards Walker, was awarded the medal for her service during the Civil War. Members of all branches of service—the Army, Navy, Marines, Air Force, and Coast Guard—have been honored.

It would be impossible to tell the stories of all the medal recipients. Instead, this book tells the stories of eleven recipients who represent the bravery and patriotism of all who have been awarded their nation's highest military honor.

Some of these—Dr. Mary Edwards Walker, Sergeant Alvin York, and Eddie Rickenbacker—became famous as medal recipients. Their names were, at least for a time, as famous as the medal itself and the wars they fought in. Others—including Jacob Parrott, Hiroshi Miyamura, and William Carney—returned home after their battles ended and sank into relative obscurity.

Two of the recipients included in this book continued serving their country in the military. One, John Bulkeley, ended his career as an admiral in the U.S. Navy. The second, Jay Vargas, retired from the

U.S. Marines as a colonel. At the time this book was written, he was working for the government in California.

More than 550 of those who were awarded medals were killed in combat. The bravery that made them medal recipients also cost them their lives. The stories of three of these heroes—Mitchell Red Cloud, a Native American who was awarded the medal for his bravery in Korea, and Randall Shughart and Gary Gordon, both awarded the medal for action in Somalia—are included in this book.

Sadly, while no sane person desires war, the nature of humankind means that wars will continue to ravage the earth. Someday that may change, and the Medal of Honor will be a relic of the past. For now, the best that we can hope for is that brave men and women like these medal recipients will continue fighting for freedom and democracy. The stories of these eleven can stand as shining examples of the courage that free people need when threatened with a loss of their freedom.

Jacob Parrott

Jacob Parrott

The First Medal Recipient

In early April of 1862, a young Union Army soldier was called from his tent in a camp in Tennessee. "My captain," he said later, ". . . asked me if I would go on a secret expedition, and told me that, if I agreed to go, I should go up to his tent . . . and report to him. I went up and told him I would go."[1]

In this way, Jacob Parrott, an eighteen-year-old private from Ohio, was chosen for what came to be known as the Andrews Raid. For his part in this raid, Parrott became the first man to receive the Medal of Honor.

At the time of the raid, the Civil War had been going on for almost one year. As the Battle of Shiloh raged in western Tennessee, two men met in the eastern part of that state, far from the fighting. One of the men, Brigadier General Ormsby Mitchel, was in command of the Union Army unit in the area. The other, James Andrews, was a Virginia native and a Union spy. That night, Andrews put forth a daring plan. He would lead two dozen men on a raid far behind the Rebel lines. They would burn bridges and tear up track on the train line between Atlanta, Georgia, and Chattanooga, Tennessee. In those days, rail lines carried almost all freight and passengers between major cities. With trains unable to reach Chattanooga from Atlanta, the Tennessee city would be cut off. It would fall to Mitchel's troops. The general wanted to capture Chattanooga. He gave his approval.

The next day, Andrews began recruiting men for his raid. Jacob Parrott was one of the first to volunteer.

Little is known of Parrott's life before he joined the army. We do know he was from Hardin County, Ohio. We know his parents were dead when he enlisted and that he was a farmer before joining the army.

On the night of Monday, April 7, Parrott and twenty-three other men met with Andrews outside Shelbyville, Tennessee. It was a wild night. The wind moaned in the trees. Lightning flashed, and thunder rumbled like the sound of far-off cannon.[2]

As the men stood on a rise near a rail track, Andrews laid out his plan. He told the raiders to travel in small groups to Marietta, Georgia, about thirty miles north of Atlanta. Dressed in civilian clothes and carrying pistols, they were to board a northbound train. He would already be on the train. At a signal from him, they would capture the train and race north with it. They would burn bridges and tear up track as they went. Andrews warned the men that if they were caught they would face death as spies. He gave them a chance to back out of the planned raid. "No one, however, showed the faintest desire to avail himself of this offer," recalled Corporal William Pittinger, one of the raiders.[3] That very night, the raiders headed south. In addition to Parrott and Andrews, the raiding party included three sergeants, Pittinger and four other corporals, fourteen privates, and one civilian, William Campbell. The soldiers were all from Ohio regiments.

Parrott and nineteen-year-old Private Samuel Robertson set out together. That night they stumbled ten miles in the darkness. They waded through knee-deep mud, soaked by a heavy rain. Finally, they took refuge in a shed. In the morning, they rose and began walking again.[4] For four days and nights, the two young men trudged through the rain across enemy territory.

In the predawn hours of April 12, Parrott and eighteen other raiders entered the Marietta train station. (Five of the men were missing. Three never made it to the depot, and two came late.) Andrews, as planned, had gone on to Atlanta. While his men were gathering in Marietta, he boarded a northbound train. At about 5 A.M., Parrott and the others bought one-way tickets to the town of Big Shanty, eight miles north. In minutes, the train from Atlanta, with Andrews on board, pulled into the station. At 5:15 A.M., with the raiders on board, it headed north, pulled by a powerful engine known as the *General.* Soon, it came to a stop in Big Shanty. The conductor called out, "Twenty minutes for breakfast."[5] When the passengers, conductor, and engineer climbed off to eat breakfast at a hotel near the station, Andrews gave his signal, and his men struck.

Quickly the raiders uncoupled the engine and three boxcars from the rest of the train. Andrews, with two men who knew how to operate an engine, got into the *General's* cab. The others climbed into the boxcars. At a nod from Andrews, the engine and cars lurched into motion. The raiders had done it! They'd stolen a rebel train!

As the raiders steamed north, they stopped the train several times. They tore up tracks and cut telegraph lines. In this way, they thought, they would delay any pursuers. They were wrong.

The *General's* engineer, Jeff Cain, conductor William Fuller, and a mechanic, Anthony Murphy, heard the train pull away from Big Shanty. They sprinted from the hotel by the tracks and ran after the train on foot. A few miles up the track, the three men found a handcart. They jumped on the cart and continued the chase. Soon they found an engine, the *Yonah,* parked on a siding, ready to roll. They leaped onto the *Yonah* and steamed after the raiders. After just a few miles, they had to abandon the *Yonah* when they came to a spot where southbound freight trains blocked their way. Soon, though, they found another engine, the *William R. Smith*. They chased after the raiders in the *Smith* until they were forced to abandon that engine as well. Still, luck was with the Southern railroad men. After running several miles up the track, they found yet another engine. It was the *Texas*.

The raiders, meanwhile, had stopped several times to wait on sidings for southbound trains to pass and then to tear up track. One of the men later said they were working on the rails when, "not far behind us we heard the scream of a locomotive bearing down on us at lightning speed."[6] It was the *Texas*, with Fuller, Murphy, and Cain on board.

The raiders jumped back on the stolen train. They raced north, toward the Union Army lines. But now the rebels were close behind. Andrews and his men threw rail ties on the tracks, trying to slow the *Texas*. Nothing worked. Finally, just five miles from the Tennessee border, the *General* ran out of fuel. Andrews told the raiders it was every man for himself. They should abandon the train and try to make their way back to the Union lines. They jumped from the train and fled into the surrounding woods.

Within a week, all the raiders who had made it to Marietta were captured, including the two who missed the train. Soon after his capture, Parrott was flogged by a Confederate officer. "I suppose, as I was

In this painting we can see what may have taken place once the *General* ran out of fuel and the raiders had to abandon the train. For his part in the raid, Jacob Parrott received the first Medal of Honor ever awarded.

the youngest, they thought they could make me [talk]; but I wouldn't tell them anything," he later said.[7]

Soon after their capture, Andrews and seven of his men were hanged as spies. One of those hanged was Private Robertson.

For a time, it looked as if all the men would be put to death. However, the rebels feared that some of their men in Union hands would be hanged if any more of the raiders were killed. They let Parrott and the other men live. In October, Parrott and the others escaped. Eight made their way to freedom, but six, including Parrott, were recaptured.

For the next five months, Parrott and the others remained in prison. Finally, in March of 1863, they were set free.

Later that month, the six freed men met with Secretary of War Edwin Stanton in Washington. With Parrott at that meeting were Pittinger, Privates William Bensinger and Robert Buffum, Sergeant Elihu Mason, and Corporal William Reddick.

Pittinger later said that Stanton "seemed especially pleased" with Parrott. The secretary offered Parrott a chance to attend West Point Military Academy. Pittinger recalled that Parrott said that he "would rather go back and fight the rebels who had used him so badly."

Stanton also told the six men they would be "great heroes" when they returned to their homes.[8] He then left the room and came back holding a

After their capture, Jacob Parrott and the other men involved in the Andrews Raid were imprisoned by the Confederacy. One such prison was this one in Andersonville, Georgia, where as many as 33,000 Union prisoners were crowded inside, forced to live in tents without medicine or clean water.

medal. Congress, he said, had ordered new medals to be prepared to honor soldiers and sailors for valor. "[Y]our party shall have the first," he said.[9] He then handed the medal to Jacob Parrott, the first man ever to be presented with the Medal of Honor.

Soon after the meeting with Stanton, Parrott went back to war. He fought in the Battle of Atlanta. Later, he took part in a great victory march in the nation's capital. After the war, he went back to Ohio, where he became a successful businessman. He died in 1912.

Eventually, almost all the raiders were given Medals of Honor. Andrews and Campbell did not get medals because they were civilians. A third raider was not honored when it was discovered that he had enlisted and served under an assumed name. Of all those men who received medals, though, Jacob Parrott has a special place in history as the first man to be awarded his nation's highest military honor.

William Carney

2

William Carney

The First African-American Recipient

Just after sunset on a hot summer evening in 1863, about six hundred African-American soldiers gathered on a beach in South Carolina. At a signal from their leader, the men marched at quick time along the shore toward a Confederate fort. As they neared the fort, the night was torn by the sounds of war. Muskets and pistols rattled. Cannon roared and shells screamed. Men howled in agony. "Every flash showed the ground dotted with men of the regiment, killed or wounded," reported Captain Luis Emilio, a survivor of that attack.[1]

As the firing from the fort continued, the African-American soldiers pressed on. A twenty-three-year-old sergeant named William Carney rushed up a slope that led to the fort's walls and planted the Stars and Stripes at the top of the slope. As the fight raged around him, Carney held his ground and kept the flag aloft. He only retreated when the other Union soldiers were driven off by the Confederate defenders. For his bravery that night, Carney became the first African-American to receive the Medal of Honor.

Carney was born in 1840 in Norfolk, Virginia. His mother, Ann, a slave, had been freed by her master at the time of his death. His freeman father, also named William, was a sailor.

Not much is known about Carney's boyhood. His childhood was almost certainly filled with hardship. It is known that at about the age of fourteen he attended a secret school operated by a minister in Norfolk. (In most places in the South before the Civil War, it was against the law for African-American children to go to school.)

When Carney was about fifteen, he and his parents moved to New Bedford, Massachusetts, where he worked for a time as a handyman. Perhaps wishing to follow the example of his teacher in Norfolk, Carney for a time considered becoming a minister. The start of the Civil War put an end to those plans.[2]

It is likely that Carney wanted to join the Union Army soon after the Civil War began on April 12, 1861. Many African Americans flocked to enlist in the army and navy in the earliest days of the war. Several tried to form all-African-American military units. For two years, though, African-American men who wanted to fight were told the war was a white-man's war. President Abraham Lincoln and other leaders in the North were fearful that arming free African Americans would only serve to strengthen the Confederacy. Allowing African Americans into the military, Lincoln said, "would turn 50,000 bayonets from the loyal Border States against us."[3]

The door to military service was finally opened to Carney and other African Americans in late 1862, when President Lincoln issued the Emancipation Proclamation. In addition to freeing slaves who lived in states that were in open rebellion against the Union, the proclamation said that free African Americans would be allowed to serve in the army and navy.

The 54th Massachusetts Infantry, formed by John Andrews, the abolitionist governor of Massachusetts, was the first black regiment formed in a free state. While the regiment's enlisted men were all black, its officers above the rank of lieutenant were whites, for the U.S. military was not yet prepared to give black men high rank. The regiment's commander was twenty-five-year-old Robert Shaw, the son of a proud Massachusetts abolitionist family.

On February 17, three days after the first call for volunteers, William Carney enlisted in the new regiment.[4]

Soon after enlisting, Carney and other enlistees from New Bedford were sent to Camp Meigs, not far from Boston. There Carney was made a sergeant. He was assigned to Company C, known as the Massachusetts Company because virtually all its men came from New Bedford.

By mid-April, the regiment was at its full strength of a thousand men comprising ten companies. For about six weeks, these volunteers trained in Massachusetts. On May 28, the 54th left for the South, headed for action.

For several weeks, the 54th operated along the coast of Georgia and South Carolina. In that time, the regiment saw little action. Then, on July 8, the 54th was ordered to join other elements of the Union Army in a battle to capture the important city of Charleston.

Taking Charleston would not be easy. The city was well guarded by Fort Sumter, built on an island in Charleston Harbor. Sumter, in turn, was guarded by Fort Wagner, located on the end of Morris Island, overlooking the harbor. Fort Wagner has been called the greatest earthwork fort ever built. Its double walls were constructed of sand and huge logs. It was armed with sixteen big guns and manned by about seventeen hundred Confederate troops, including battle-hardened veterans.

The men of the 54th first took positions on James Island near Charleston. There, on July 15, four of the regiment's companies engaged rebel troops in a fierce skirmish. In the fighting that day, the 54th was credited with saving the lives of hundreds of

The capture of Fort Sumter by Confederate forces marked the start of the Civil War.

white soldiers of the 10th Connecticut Infantry. Carney and the other men of Company C, however, were not involved in the fighting.

Following the action on James Island, the regiment and other Union Army units moved to Morris Island to take part in an all-out assault on Fort Wagner. On Morris Island, General George C. Strong, commander of the brigade that included the 54th, told Colonel Shaw that his men could lead the attack. Shaw immediately ordered the 54th to get ready to charge the fort.

As the sun set on July 18, the officers and men of the 54th waited nervously on the shore of Morris Island for the signal to begin the assault. A few men joked, but most were tight-lipped, quiet.[5]

At 7:45 P.M., the signal to attack was given. Colonel Shaw unsheathed his sword. "Move in quick time until within a hundred yards of the fort, then double quick and charge!" he ordered. He led the regiment in the march to the fort, and into history.[6]

When the marching men were about two hundred yards from the fort, the rebels opened fire. "A sheet of flame, followed by a running fire, like electric sparks, swept along the parapet," one of the men later said. The men of the 54th, most of whom had never been in combat before, were raked by deadly small arms and cannon fire from two directions. Scores of men were instantly killed or wounded. Shaw raised his sword in a signal to charge. The regiment rushed through a hail of bullets and exploding shells, across a moat filled waist-deep with water, and toward the fort's thick, sloping, earthwork walls.[7]

William Carney was among the first group to near the fort. He ran through a hail of screaming bullets and exploding shells. At his side ran Sergeant John Wall, carrying the regiment's national colors. Suddenly, a cannon shell exploded nearby. Wall was blown into the air. Before the flagstaff slipped from the wounded man's grasp, Carney grabbed the flag. Ducking and dodging, he ran up the earthwork slope. As he neared the parapet, he was shot in the thigh. He fell to his knees, but managed to plant the Stars and Stripes atop the parapet. For more than an hour, Carney knelt on the earthwork, holding the flag high as men fell all around him.

For a time, the brave men of the shattered 54th battled on against overwhelming odds. They might have taken the fort that night, but reinforcements were late in arriving. Finally, the men of the 54th had to fall back.

Carney, still holding the colors, clawed his way down the slope from the parapet. As he retreated, he was shot twice more. Still he struggled on until finally, with the help of a white soldier, he reached a field hospital behind the Union Army lines.

As Carney entered the hospital, still clutching the Stars and Stripes, wounded men cheered him. Exhausted and bleeding, he collapsed to the ground. "Boys, the old flag never touched the ground," he exclaimed as he fell.[8]

After he finished his military service, William Carney was employed as a U. S. postal worker for thirty years.

In the attack, the regiment suffered terrible losses. Two hundred fifty-six were killed, wounded, or listed as missing in action. One of the dead was Colonel Shaw, shot through the heart as he stood atop the parapet with his sword raised high.

Carney survived the battle. Discharged because of his wounds, he was a hero. Ultimately, William Carney received the Medal of Honor for his bravery in the midst of the battle for Fort Wagner. The flag he saved that night and so bravely guarded was enshrined in the Massachusetts State House, where it is still on display today.

Following the Civil War, Carney briefly lived in California. He then returned to New Bedford, where he worked as a mail carrier for more than thirty years. In 1901, following his retirement from the postal service, he moved to Boston, where he took a job as a messenger in the State House. William Carney, the first African American to receive his nation's highest military award, died on December 9, 1908.

Mary Edwards Walker

3

Mary Edwards Walker

Civil War Doctor

In the fall of 1865, not long after the end of the Civil War, Dr. Mary Edwards Walker was awarded the Medal of Honor. So far, she is the only woman ever to receive her nation's highest military honor. The order granting Walker her medal read, in part:

> Dr. Mary E. Walker . . . has devoted herself with much patriotic zeal to the sick and wounded soldiers, both in the field and hospitals . . . and has also endured hardships as a prisoner of war four months in a Southern prison. . . .
>
> Whereas, in the opinion of the President . . . recognition of her services and sufferings should be made:
>
> It is ordered . . . that the usual medal of honor for meritorious service be given her. . . . [1]

Mary Walker was born on November 26, 1832, in the town of Oswego, on the banks of Lake Erie in New York State. Mary had four older sisters and one younger brother. Her father was a carpenter. He was also a self-taught doctor and teacher. Her mother's ancestors were some of the first settlers in New England.

Mary's father and mother taught her that she was as good as any boy. Her father loved books and knew the value of school. He urged Mary to learn a profession. This was a strange idea for those long-ago days. He had other ideas that were strange, as well. He believed the corsets worn by women in those days were bad for their health. He would not allow Mary and her sisters to wear corsets around the family's farm.[2]

As a girl, Mary was a student in the local school where her parents taught. She also studied her father's medical books and soon resolved that she would become a doctor.[3] In late 1853, at the age of twenty-one, she enrolled in a medical college not far from her home. In those days, it took just two years to become a doctor, not the six or more years it takes today. Late the next year, Mary Walker finished school. She became one of the first women doctors in America.

It was hard for Walker to get patients. Many people thought she was strange because she was a dress reformer. She and other members of the dress reform movement believed the long, heavy skirts worn by most women in those days were not healthy. Instead of a dress, Mary Walker wore a version of the Bloomerite costume made famous by Amelia Bloomer. Mary's outfit was a dress that hung to her knees worn over a pair of trousers. She still wore no corset. Later in her life she said that her waist had "never been confined in one of those steel traps."[4]

Not long after she became a doctor, Mary Walker wed one of her classmates, Dr. Albert Miller. The ceremony was performed with the word "obey" taken out of the marriage vows. "How barbarous the very idea of one equal promising to be the slave of another instead of both entering life's greatest drama as intelligent, equal parties," she said.[5] The marriage ended in a divorce about five years later.

When the Civil War began, Walker was living and working in Rome, New York. Because of the war there was a great need for doctors. Soon after the battle of Bull Run (the first great battle of the war) in July 1861, Walker went to Washington, D.C., where she volunteered to serve as an army doctor.

Army officials didn't know what to make of Mary Walker. Time after time her request to serve as an army surgeon was turned down. Still, with sick and wounded soldiers on every hand, she was able to make herself useful. She worked as a volunteer in a hospital set up in the Patent Office building in Washington and in field hospitals in nearby Virginia.

In the autumn of 1863, Walker went south, closer to the fighting. She arrived in Chattanooga,

Tennessee, in September, as thousands of wounded from the Battle of Chickamauga were flowing into the city. Her service appears to have attracted the notice of Union General George H. Thomas.[6] Not long after her arrival, the general told her to report to the commanding officer of the 52nd Ohio Infantry Regiment. She was to be the regiment's assistant surgeon.

Walker was not welcome at her new job. The regiment's medical director called her "a medical monstrosity."[7] He ordered a medical board to examine her qualifications. The board, comprised of male doctors, said she was not fit to serve as a doctor. This was not surprising since most men (and many women) thought, as one doctor wrote in 1859, "The duties of the physician are contrary and opposed to [a woman's] moral, intellectual and physical nature."[8]

Even without the board's approval, Walker went to work. The regiment was in camp, not in battle, and its men were healthy. There was not much for her to do around camp, so she visited civilians in the area, providing care to them. On April 10, 1864, while Walker was on one of her trips outside the camp, she was captured by a Confederate patrol. The rebels thought she was a spy.

For the next four months, Walker was held prisoner in Richmond, Virginia. Even as a prisoner, she refused to bend her dress reform principles. When one of her guards said he might be "sympathetic" to her if she would dress like other women,

Walker refused. She continued to wear her short dress over trousers, and her blue uniform jacket.[9]

On August 12, Walker was released as part of a prisoner exchange. Later she was to brag that while her own army gave her only grudging recognition, the rebels knew her true worth. After all, she'd been exchanged "man for man" for a Confederate major.[10]

After her release, Walker finally got the official notice she wanted. She was awarded a contract as Acting Assistant Surgeon, United States Army, with a salary of $100 per month. As a so-called contract surgeon, she was not a regular member of the army. Walker's first job was to care for women in a prison in Kentucky. In March of 1865, just a few weeks before the end of the war, she was moved to Clarkesville, Tennessee, where she was placed in charge of an orphanage. She was in Clarkesville when the war came to an end. About eight months later, Mary Walker was awarded her Medal of Honor.

Dr. Mary Walker's story was not over, though. For the rest of her life she worked for dress reform and for women's rights. She spoke to lawmakers in Washington and around the nation, trying to win equal rights for women. She lectured in England and across America and wrote about voting rights and dress reform. She never turned her back on what she believed, even though she was laughed at because of the way she dressed.

In 1916, the U.S. Army set up a panel to review all the Medal of Honor awards presented over the

Mary Edwards Walker is still the only woman to receive the Medal of Honor.

years. At that time, 2,625 medals had been handed out. The review board determined that 911 of those medals were undeserved. Mary Edwards Walker's name was stricken from the roll of medal recipients. As a contract surgeon, the army said, she had not been a sworn member of the military.[11]

Walker responded aggressively. The government, she said, might strip her of the honor, but it would never take her medals. (She had her original medal from 1865 along with a second, newer design she had received in 1906.) For the rest of her life, she proudly wore one of her medals every day.[12]

In early 1917, at the age of eighty-four, Walker slipped and fell as she was climbing the steps of the Capitol Building in Washington. Old and frail, she never recovered. She died in Oswego on February 21, 1919, at the age of eighty-six.

In the mid-1970s, as American society began looking more closely at women's issues, many women asked that the government review Walker's eligibility for the Medal of Honor. The Army Board of Correction of Military Records in 1977 determined that if Walker had not been a woman she would have been commissioned as an army officer in 1861. Board members cited her "acts of distinguished gallantry, self-sacrifice, patriotism, dedication and unflinching loyalty to her country," and recommended that her medal be reinstated.[13] On June 10, 1977, Mary Edwards Walker's Medal of Honor was restored.

Eddie Rickenbacker

4

Eddie Rickenbacker
World War I Ace of Aces

On April 29, 1918, an American airman climbed into an airplane on a field in western France. In minutes, he was airborne, flying high over the border between the warring nations of France and Germany. Suddenly, he spotted a lone German airplane. "I was on his tail in an instant," the American flyer later said. "I held the triggers down. I could see the stream of fire climbing up the fuselage and into the pilot's seat. I watched the [German plane] curve down and crash. I had brought down my first enemy airplane."[1]

That American pilot was twenty-seven-year-old Edward ("Eddie") Rickenbacker. He had been in France for less than a month. He was a member of one of the American flying squadrons on the Western Front, the line of battle between the German forces and Allied forces in World War I. In the months that followed that first fight, Rickenbacker shot down twenty-five more German aircraft. He became America's "Ace of Aces" in World War I. For his valor as a fighter pilot, he was awarded the Congressional Medal of Honor.

Eddie Rickenbacker was born October 8, 1890, in Columbus, Ohio. His father, William Richenbacher, and mother, Elisabeth Basler, were immigrants from Switzerland. (Rickenbacker changed the spelling of his last name during the war years because the new spelling seemed less German.)[2] Eddie was the third of seven children. He had four brothers and two sisters.

In 1904, when Eddie was thirteen, his father, a construction worker, was killed at work. Eddie immediately quit school and went to work to help support his mother and his brothers and sisters. Since child labor laws required workers to be at least fourteen, he lied about his age. His first job was in a glass factory in Columbus. He worked six nights each week, from 6 P.M. to 6 A.M., for $3.50 per week.[3] Tiring of working all night, Eddie quit after a few weeks. He got a better-paying job in a steel casting factory, then worked in a brewery putting lids on beer bottles, and in a shop carving headstones for graves.

In those days, horseless carriages (early automobiles) were just beginning to be seen on the streets and dirt roads of America. One day, when he was about fourteen, Eddie got to go for a ride in a Ford runabout. Soon, he knew he wanted to be a part of the world of automobiles.[4] For a time, he worked cleaning a shop where cars were built. He then became a salesman, and later a branch manager for a Columbus automaker.

In those years, Rickenbacker not only loved working on cars, he also loved driving them, the faster the better. By 1910, he was a winning race car driver. He drove in the famed Indianapolis 500 race three times and set a world record for speed in an auto when he drove 134 miles per hour on the sand at Daytona Beach, Florida. As a race car driver, Rickenbacker survived several close calls and became famous as the Dutch Demon and the Speedy Swiss.[5]

On an October day in 1916, Rickenbacker was driving near Riverside, California, when he saw an airplane parked on a field. He drove close to the plane. As he parked, a young man walked up to his car. The young man was Glenn Martin, an airplane designer and builder who had worked for the Wright brothers. Now he was building a two-seater bomber for the U.S. Navy. As Rickenbacker inspected the airplane, Martin asked if he would like to go for a ride. "The whole flight was fascinating,"[6] Rickenbacker later said. From that day, flying was a central part of Rickenbacker's life.

During those years, the Allies (England, France, and Russia) were waging war with the Central

Powers (Germany, Austria-Hungary, and Turkey) in what was called then the Great War and has come to be known as World War I. That war started in 1914, after the murder, by a Serbian student, of the Archduke Francis Ferdinand, the heir apparent to the throne of the old monarchy of Austria-Hungary. In response to his murder, Austria-Hungary declared war on Serbia. Soon almost all the nations of Europe were at war. It was not until February 1917, when Germany declared that no ships would be safe from submarine attack, that the United States entered the war.

In the summer of that year, Rickenbacker volunteered for duty. He was sent to France to serve as a driver. There he met Colonel William (Billy) Mitchell, one of the great American pioneers in aviation. With Mitchell's help, Rickenbacker started flight training. To become a pilot, he had to lie about his age, just as he had when he was a boy looking for his first job. This time, though, he had to say he was younger than his twenty-six years.

In early 1918, after a year spent as an engineering officer, Rickenbacker was sent to gunnery school, where he learned how to shoot a machine gun mounted on an airplane. In March of that year, he was assigned to the 94th Aero Pursuit Squadron, which later became known as the Hat-in-the-Ring Squadron. It got that name from the American saying that a man would "throw his hat in the ring" if he was ready to fight.

At twenty-seven years old Rickenbacker was older than most American pilots. It was in this Spad biplane that Rickenbacker went up aganst his German foes.

Rickenbacker soon became the most famous pilot in the squadron. The skills that had served him so well as a race car driver, as well as his bravery, stood him in good stead as a fighter pilot. Following his first victory in late April, he quickly notched four more. He was an ace, a pilot with five confirmed victories, or kills. For that accomplishment, the French government rewarded Rickenbacker with one of its highest military honors, the Croix de Guerre (Cross of War).

For the next month, Rickenbacker honed his fighting skills on one mission after another. He became a crafty hunter. One morning before daylight he took off and flew behind the German lines. He circled high over an airfield and cut his engine to glide as silent as a hawk. Suddenly, he saw three German planes, known as Albatrosses, taking off. For a time, Rickenbacker tailed the three German planes. Then, without warning, he dropped out of the sky to attack the rearmost aircraft. "At fifty yards I gave him a ten-second burst of machine gun fire. I saw the bullets hit the back of [the pilot's] seat," he later said. "The scared [German] had made a stupid mistake in diving rather than trying to outmaneuver me."[7]

Rickenbacker himself had several close calls. He also saw several of his friends killed in combat. One of his comrades, Raoul Lufbery, died when he jumped, without a parachute, from his burning plane. From that day forward, Rickenbacker tried to convince the military authorities to issue parachutes

Eddie Rickenbacker had been a race car driver before he became a fighter pilot. Here we can see the insignia of the famous Hat-in-the-Ring Squadron.

to flyers. His efforts were unsuccessful, though. If pilots had parachutes, the government said, they would abandon their expensive aircraft rather than fight to bring them home safely.

For a time during the summer of 1918, Rickenbacker was out of combat. He was sick with an ear infection that made flying in a plane with an open cockpit pure torture. By September, he was back in action. He quickly got several more kills. On September 24, he was named commander of the famed Hat-in-the-Ring Squadron. The next morning, he took off early on a one-man mission. Flying one of the squadron's new Spad 13 airplanes—a sleek, fast-diving fighter built in France—he sped west. Over the French town of Verdun, he saw a flight of seven enemy aircraft. Two of the planes were two-seater reconnaissance (spy) planes. The other five were Type 5 Fokkers, the most famous of all the German fighter planes. Hidden in the glare of the rising sun, he allowed the German planes to fly below him. "I cut back the engine and dived silently on the last Fokker," he said later. "He [the pilot] glanced behind him at the same moment that I pressed my triggers. He tried to pull away, and that was his last living act."[8] After downing the fighter, Rickenbacker turned his attention on the photographic planes. In minutes, he downed one of those.

For that double kill, Eddie Rickenbacker was later awarded the Congressional Medal of Honor. As was often the case for Medal recipients after both the

Civil War and World War I, before the armed services were able to efficiently keep records of what happened in battles, Rickenbacker did not receive his award for some time. When he did receive his award in 1930, he said he viewed the medal as "a true tribute to my comrades-in-arms, soldiers and sailors, living and dead."[9]

Following the September 1918 air battle for which Rickenbacker was awarded the Medal of Honor, he went on to record a total of twenty-six victories, an air combat record that stood until World War II, when it was broken by U.S. Marine Pilot Richard Bong.

Rickenbacker's adventurous life continued after the war. He was copilot aboard a plane that set a new speed record in a 1934 flight between California and New Jersey. In 1938, he became the first president of Eastern Airlines. In 1941, he survived a plane crash in Atlanta. The next year, he survived a crash at sea and spent twenty-four days adrift in a life raft with seven companions. Eddie Rickenbacker died in 1973 at the age of eighty-two.

Alvin York

Alvin York

Conscientious Objector and War Hero

In the late fall of 1917, a thirty-year-old man climbed a mountain near the town of Pall Mall in Tennessee. He was a troubled man. He was sick at heart because he had been called to serve in the U.S. Army in the First World War. That meant he would have to go against his religious beliefs and kill other men. For two days and nights, the man stayed on top of the mountain. He prayed and asked for guidance from his God. At the end of his time in prayer, he walked down from the mountain. He was a changed man. He was ready to fight. He was, he said, a "soldier of the Lord."[1]

That soldier of the Lord was Alvin York. As a corporal and later a sergeant with the famed All-American

Division in France during World War I, he was to become one of the most famous soldiers of all time.

Alvin York was born on December 13, 1887, in Pall Mall. The son of backwoods people, York spent plenty of time hunting as a boy. He became a crack shot, able to hit the head of a nail at a hundred yards. He also spent much of his youth drinking moonshine (illegal, homemade alcohol), gambling, and "raising hell" in the hills near his home.[2] In 1915, though, he turned his back on his wild life. He became a member of the Church of Christ in Christian Union. This was a pacifist church; its members did not believe in war.

Soon after the United States entered the war in April 1917, men all across the country were drafted for duty. In the fall of that year, York was ordered to report for military duty. At first, the Tennessean tried to avoid going to war. He claimed what is known as conscientious objector status. He said his religious beliefs made it impossible for him to fight.[3] Four times he asked for exemptions to his draft orders. Four times his request was denied.

In the fall of 1917, soon after his last request was refused, he was ordered to report for duty. Reluctantly, he did as he was told. Soon, he was sent to Camp Gordon, Georgia, for training. There, he was assigned to Company G, 328th Infantry, 82nd Division. Known as the All-American Division because its men came from all parts of the country, the 82nd was a combat unit destined to see battle.

Once he knew he was headed for combat, York told his commanding officer, Major George Buxton, he did not know if he could kill another man, even an enemy. Buxton was himself a devout Christian who soon realized that York was a sincere believer. Buxton and York spent a long night discussing the Bible's teachings. The major asked York if he believed the Bible. "Every sentence, every word," York answered.[4] Buxton then reminded the mountain man that Christ had said, "He that hath no sword, let him sell his cloak and buy one" (Luke 22.36). He reminded York that Jesus chased the money lenders from the temple. Would Jesus not fight to protect people from the Germans and their allies, he asked?[5]

Following his long talk with Buxton, York was more confused than ever. He asked his commander for a pass so he could return home and decide what to do. He arrived home on March 21, 1918, and he fled to the mountains to think and pray. When he came down, he was convinced that God wanted him to fight. He was also certain God would protect him in battle.[6] Indeed, once convinced that he was doing the right thing by being a soldier, he threw himself into the military life with the same kind of zeal that marked his life as a Christian.

On May 1, 1918, York and his division sailed for France. "[W]e were to be peacemakers. . . . We were to help make peace, the only way the Germans would understand," York later said.[7]

In late June, after a few weeks preparing for combat, the mountain man and his fellow soldiers were ordered to the front. They were sent to the Argonne Forest near the town of Cunel in northeast France. York and the other men in the 82nd got their first taste of heavy combat in September when the Division attacked German positions along the front. York led a squad in an assault on the small village of Norroy. York later said the four days of fighting before Norroy fell were "heartbreaking for a simple country boy." He hated, he added, "to see all of those good Americans lying around."[8] In the assault, the Germans attacked the Americans with poisonous mustard gas. As York watched, men around him went crazy from the strain of combat, tore off their gas masks, and died. Others were mowed down by machine-gun fire or killed by artillery. While the experience shook York, he found peace in his faith. The only thing he could do, he wrote in his diary, was "pray and trust God."[9]

The attack against Norroy was part of a major Allied offensive against the German forces massed in the Meuse-Argonne area of eastern France. On October 8, as part of that drive by the American, British, and French armies, York and fifteen other men of his regiment were ordered to attack a German machine-gun battalion. Led by Sergeant Bernard Early, the sixteen soldiers crawled on their bellies to the rear of the machine-gun nests. They rushed one of the enemy positions, capturing several officers and men. Suddenly, a hillside above York and the others erupted in machine-gun fire. Other Germans had turned their guns on the Americans. Six of the men with York were killed outright. Three, including Sergeant Early, were wounded. Bullets passed so close to York they burned his face.

With Early wounded, York took command. He went on the offensive. He quickly saw that the machine gunners had to raise their heads to aim down the hill at him. Using his rifle, he picked off one after another of the German machine gunners. Soon none dared raise his head to aim down the hill. Suddenly, from a line of bushes to York's left, a German officer and a half-dozen men rushed his position with their bayonets at the ready. Calmly, using an automatic pistol, York shot the last man in the group of attackers. He then shot the next to last, and so on. Later, he explained that this was how he shot wild turkeys at home, so the ones in front didn't know the ones behind were being killed.[10]

Finally, the German lieutenant in command of that section of the German machine-gun line had had enough; about twenty of his men had been killed by York. He stood and signaled for his men to cease firing. In seconds, all the Germans dropped their weapons except one soldier who threw a small grenade in York's direction. The throw missed, and York shot the man and killed him.[11]

Soon, York and his six unwounded companions took their captured foes at gunpoint back toward the

Four months after capturing 132 Germans in the Argonne Forest, York returned to show where the action took place. At the end of the war, the state of Tennessee gave York a farm to reward his bravery.

Allied lines. As the group marched down the hillside, York and his men captured more and more Germans. Only one enemy soldier tried to fight back, and, once again, York used his pistol to end the threat.

Upon reaching division headquarters behind the lines, York's catch of enemy prisoners was counted. He'd bagged 128 enlisted men and four officers. "Well, York, I hear you have captured the whole damned German army," an officer said.

York saluted and said no, he'd only captured 132 men.[12]

When Alvin York marched with his prisoners out of the Argonne Forest, he became an instant hero not only to the American people but to America's allies. He was given medals by both the French and Italian governments. Almost immediately, he was promoted to sergeant and awarded the Distinguished Service Cross by the Americans. About three months later, after his exploits were investigated, he was awarded the Medal of Honor. Across America he was hailed as the greatest soldier to wear a uniform in the Great War.

After the war, York returned to the hills he'd always known as home. He and his wife, the daughter of a neighboring farmer, had eight children. He worked as a farmer and blacksmith, just as he'd done before he was called to war. He preached in the local church. In 1964, Alvin York died at the age of seventy-six. He was buried in the family graveyard in Pall Mall. There were 8,000 mourners in attendance.

John Bulkeley

6

John Bulkeley
The Hero of the Philippines

In the predawn hours of a January day in 1942, two U.S. Navy patrol torpedo (PT) boats, crept into Subic Bay on the Philippine island of Luzon. Just a few weeks earlier, the Japanese had attacked the big navy base at Pearl Harbor. That action drew the United States into World War II. Now the American sailors on the PT boats were ready to strike back. They hoped to attack two enemy ships they knew were anchored in the bay.

Inside the bay, the two small boats slid through the night. Suddenly, the men aboard one of the boats spied the silhouette of a large ship about five hundred yards ahead. It could only be the enemy vessel. Lieutenant John Bulkeley, the boat's skipper, eased her close to the Japanese ship. The Americans were about to strike when a light on the enemy ship flashed on. The light flashed a coded message asking the PT boat to identify itself. "We answered, all right," Lieutenant Bulkeley later said, "with two torpedoes."[1]

As soon as the torpedoes were launched, Bulkeley turned the PT boat sharply to starboard (the right). He pushed her throttles to full speed. As the boat raced for safety, a huge explosion sent a fireball rolling into the sky behind it. PT 34, with Bulkeley in command, had registered the first kill made by a PT boat in World War II. For his actions that night and during the next several months, Bulkeley would ultimately be awarded the Medal of Honor. By the war's end, he would be one of America's greatest heroes.

Bulkeley was born on August 19, 1911, in New York City. One of his ancestors was second in command aboard John Paul Jones's ship, the *Bonhomme Richard*. Another was a midshipman aboard British Lord Horatio Nelson's flagship, the *Victory*, at the battle of Trafalgar. It was little wonder, then, that by the time Bulkeley was twelve he was spending his summers working as a deckhand on cargo ships in the Caribbean.[2]

Following his graduation from high school in 1928, Bulkeley attended the United States Naval Academy at Annapolis. He graduated in 1933.

When Bulkeley graduated, the nation was in the grip of the Great Depression. As a way to cut costs, the navy did not grant commissions to graduates, including Bulkeley, who were in the bottom half of their class. Then, in 1935, the navy had a change of heart. Bulkeley was called to active duty and was given a commission as an ensign.

Soon after he was commissioned, Bulkeley was sent to China, where he served for about four years. There, on November 10, 1938, he married Alice Wood.

Early the next year, Bulkeley and his wife came back to the United States. He was ordered to serve on the aircraft carrier *Saratoga*. After about a year on the carrier, he was put in charge of a squadron of PT boats.

By the time Bulkeley was made skipper of his squadron, much of the world was at war. Germany was at war with its neighbors. Japan was laying waste to China. President Franklin Roosevelt wanted to be ready if Japan attacked the Philippines. He called General Douglas MacArthur out of retirement. MacArthur was the former chief of staff of the U.S. Army.

MacArthur soon set up headquarters in the Philippines. He began building a force to repel the expected invasion by Japan. In August 1941, Bulkeley was sent to the Philippines as part of that buildup. He was put in command of Motor Torpedo Boat Squadron 3, with six PT boats.

PT boats were known as mosquito boats. They were small wooden vessels, designed for high-speed attacks at close range. About seventy-five feet in length, each was armed with machine guns and four torpedoes in tubes. In Bulkeley's words, the PT boats were "little eggshells, designed to roar in, let fly a Sunday punch, and then get the hell out. . . ."[3]

As soon as the thirty-year-old Bulkeley and his squadron arrived in Manila, he made his boats ready for war. "Our decks are cleared. If Japan wants war, we are ready," he wrote to his wife in early November.[4] Just over a month later, the Japanese attacked the U.S. Navy Base at Pearl Harbor. The United States was at war.

Two days after the attack on Pearl Harbor, the Japanese attacked Luzon. When that attack ended, the U.S. forces in the Philippines were all but destroyed. Bulkeley had sent the six boats in his squadron into open waters, though. His little fleet was unharmed. It was also about all that remained of the U.S. Navy in the Far East, but it was ready to fight. On the night of January 19, 1942, Bulkeley and his men staged their daring raid on the Japanese ship in Subic Bay.

Within days of that raid, Bulkeley was a hero. His picture was on the front page of the *New York Daily News*. A huge headline screamed, "Mosquito Raider Torpedoes Ship."[5]

Within two weeks, Bulkeley's boats had sunk two more Japanese ships. In the weeks that followed, he and his men made one foray after another against the enemy. They battled not only the Japanese, but also

Bulkeley decided to make the Navy his career. Achieving the rank of Vice Admiral, he became one of the most decorated Naval officers.

a shortage of supplies for their boats and of food for themselves.

During these weeks, American troops were besieged on the Bataan Peninsula, overlooking Manila Bay. Other troops were under attack on the tiny island of Corregidor, where General MacArthur and his family had taken refuge. President Franklin Roosevelt knew the Philippines would soon fall. Fearing that MacArthur might be captured, Roosevelt ordered him to leave the islands. He instructed MacArthur to go to Australia, where he would be able to make plans to retake the Philippines. The general reluctantly made plans to obey the President's orders.

In late February, MacArthur met with Bulkeley. "General MacArthur said he wanted my PT boats to . . . carry him and his party some 580 miles south," Bulkeley recalled. "I replied, 'General, it'll be a piece of cake!'"[6]

On March 11, at about 7:30 P.M., the general, his wife, and their son climbed aboard Bulkeley's PT 41. With them were a nursemaid and several other officers. Swiftly, the boat joined three other PT boats off Corregidor. (Two of the squadron's boats had been lost in the weeks following the bombing of Luzon.) Soon, the small fleet headed south. All told, the boats carried twenty passengers.

As lookouts watched for enemy destroyers, the boats made their way south through huge, wind-whipped waves. One of the boats broke down and was left behind to be picked up later. The three remaining boats pushed on. After a brief stop in a small bay, about halfway through the voyage, PT 41 and one other boat pressed on. The third boat had engine trouble and was left behind. For a second night, the little boats roared south. Several times that night, Bulkeley and the other skipper shut down their engines and drifted as Japanese warships passed close by. Finally, at about dawn on March 13, a lookout spotted an island dead ahead. Bulkeley had brought General MacArthur and the others safely to Mindanao. From there they were able to fly to Australia. "Johnny," the general said as he stepped from the boat, "you've taken me out of the jaws of death—and I won't forget it!"[7]

For the next several months, Bulkeley and his squadron—now down to just three boats—continued to harass enemy shipping. One by one in these weeks, the squadron's boats were lost. One was sunk after it was damaged in an attack. Another was set afire to keep it out of enemy hands. Then, during the second week of April 1942, Bulkeley's boat was destroyed in an air raid.

Following the loss of his last boat, Bulkeley was ordered to report to Australia. He didn't want to leave, but orders were orders, so he departed. The men Bulkeley left behind were forced to flee as the Japanese overran the islands. Some joined guerrillas fighting in the countryside. Thirty-eight of eighty-three were taken prisoner. A few, including the three

General Douglas MacArthur upon making his return to the Philippines. John Bulkeley commanded the squadron of torpedo boats that had led Gen. MacArthur to safety when the Philippine Islands were being taken by the Japanese.

skippers who had aided in MacArthur's escape, were airlifted to safety.

From Australia, Bulkeley was flown to America, where he was promoted to lieutenant commander, a rank equal to that of major in the Army. He was also given a hero's welcome. Then, on August 4, 1942, he was awarded the Congressional Medal of Honor in a special ceremony at the White House.

Bulkeley later returned to combat and played an active part in the D-day invasion of Normandy. Later still, he commanded a destroyer. He went on to serve his country until his retirement as vice admiral in 1987. By the time he retired, he had been awarded—in addition to the Medal of Honor—the Navy Cross, two Army Distinguished Service Crosses, two Silver Stars, three Distinguished Service Medals, two Legion of Merit awards, two Purple Hearts, and the Philippines Distinguished Conduct Star. He died on April 6, 1996, at the age of eighty-four.[8]

Mitchell Red Cloud

7

Mitchell Red Cloud
Ho-Chunk Warrior

The night was cold and quiet in the hills near the Chonhyon River in North Korea. American soldiers knelt in foxholes and shivered in sleeping bags in their positions on a hill north of the river. Though it was peaceful, the men knew the peace and quiet would not last. They knew the hills all around them were swarming with enemy soldiers waiting to attack.

Shortly before dawn the next morning, a guard heard a noise or sensed movement in the undergrowth near his position. "Here they come!" he cried.[1]

In seconds, as one soldier on the hill that night later said, "all hell broke loose."[2] The sky was lit by tracer rounds from enemy guns. The air was torn by the sound of exploding mortar rounds and grenades. Hundreds of screaming enemy troops streamed from the darkness toward the Americans.

The guard who sounded the alarm that November morning was twenty-five-year-old Mitchell Red Cloud, Jr. Red Cloud, called "Chief" by his Army buddies, was a veteran soldier. He'd seen action with the U.S. Marines in World War II. He was to die in the fight that early morning. But before he gave his life for his country, he was to exhibit bravery that earned him his nation's highest military honor, the Medal of Honor.

Mitchell Red Cloud, Jr. was born on July 2, 1924, near the little town of Hatfield in central Wisconsin. His father, Mitchell Red Cloud, Sr., and his mother, Nellie, were respected members of the Wisconsin-Winnebago tribe. (This tribe is now called the Ho-Chunk tribe by its members.) The elder Red Cloud served in the Army during World War I and in the peace that followed. Near the end of his life, he wrote regular columns for local newspapers in Wisconsin. Though he had only an eighth-grade education, he "used the English of a Harvard professor," according to a newspaper publisher with whom he worked.[3]

Not much is known about Mitchell Jr.'s early life. We don't even know for sure how many brothers and sisters he had. We think his family was large, as many Winnebago families were. The Red Clouds were homesteaders. They lived on a plot of land between a Christian mission that served the tribe and the town of Hatfield. We do know Mitchell Jr. was shy and quiet as a boy.[4] He attended the Neillsville Indian School, public schools near his home, and Black River Falls High School. He must not have enjoyed school very much, for in August of 1941, one month after his seventeenth birthday, he asked his father's permission to quit school. Soon after that, with his father's approval, he enlisted in the U.S. Marines.

After his training, Red Cloud was sent to fight in what was known, in World War II, as the Pacific Theater of Operations. There he joined Carlson's Raiders, a group of marines trained to wage war behind enemy lines. On November 4 of the next year, he and the other raiders landed on the coast of the island of Guadalcanal. This island, about one thousand miles northeast of Australia, was the scene of some of the worst fighting of the war. For thirty days, Red Cloud and the other marines hacked their way through the thick jungle. In that time, they were in a dozen battles with Japanese soldiers. They inflicted heavy casualties on the enemy while losing just sixteen of their own men.

Later that same year, Red Cloud caught malaria. In January 1943, he was sent home for medical treatment. Though he was offered a medical discharge, Red Cloud refused it. He wanted to stay in the Marines, even if it meant a return to combat. In December 1944, he returned to the Far East, where he served in Okinawa and the Ryukyu Islands near Japan. He was discharged in 1945, having been awarded two Purple Hearts. (The Purple Heart is the medal given to a soldier, sailor, or airman who is wounded in action.)

That Red Cloud would earn medals in battle probably came as no surprise to his family and friends in Wisconsin. After all, the Winnebago tribe believed that its men were meant to be brave in battle. The blood of great warriors ran in Red Cloud's veins. His mother was descended from Chief Winneshiek, a great Native American leader who was decorated for bravery by General George Washington. His father was a descendant of Chee-Wote-Tay-He-Ga, a warrior who lived in the early eighteenth century.[5]

After his return to Wisconsin following the war, Red Cloud wasn't happy.[6] His unhappiness may have been caused by the lack of opportunity for Native Americans near his home. In any case, he left home again. He joined the U.S. Army.

In the years right after World War II, Korea, the peninsula on the Asian mainland to the west of Japan, became a divided nation. The northern half of the country was under communist rule. This part of Korea was known as the Democratic People's Republic of Korea. The southern half of Korea was a free nation. It was known as the Republic of Korea, or South Korea. At about the time Mitchell Red Cloud joined the army, hostility between the two Koreas

Mitchell Red Cloud wearing a ceremonial head dress. Red Cloud was part of the Ho-Chunk people and was elected to the National Indian Hall of Fame because of his bravery in battle.

was growing. That hostility became open warfare on June 25, 1950. On that day, about eighty thousand North Korean soldiers invaded the South. Within days, American troops were involved in the fight. Mitchell Red Cloud was one of those soldiers. He was assigned to Company E, 19th Infantry Regiment, 24th Infantry Division.

At first, communist forces from the north were able to thrust deep into South Korean territory. By late October, however, those forces had been pushed back north to the Yalu River, which forms the border between Korea and China. There, unknown to the Americans and the United Nations forces that were their allies, the North Korean soldiers were reinforced by almost 200,000 soldiers from Communist China, ready to join the fray.

By the night of November 4, 1950, Mitchell Red Cloud, Jr. and the other men in Company E knew they were facing a fight with a large communist force. For several days they had been involved in a running battle. Enemy forces, said Red Cloud's company commander, "were in, on the flanks of, and behind the company position."[7] That night, Red Cloud was assigned to guard duty about a hundred yards from E Company's headquarters on a hill the soldiers called Hill 123. The sky was just beginning to lighten in the east when he sounded his warning to his comrades.

As enemy soldiers rushed his position, Red Cloud jumped to his feet. He opened fire with a heavy Browning Automatic Rifle. Behind him, his comrades struggled to wake and get out of their sleeping bags. Almost immediately, Red Cloud was hit by enemy fire and knocked to the ground. Bravely, he pulled himself to his feet. He wrapped one arm around a nearby tree. Holding the tree for support, he directed "accurate and intense" rifle fire at the scores of enemy soldiers who were rushing his position.[8] He continued firing until his position was overrun by the enemy, and he was killed.

Mitchell Red Cloud's actions that early morning briefly halted the attack on Company E. Thanks to him, his comrades had time to mount a hasty defense and even carry some wounded away. While the company was ultimately driven from Hill 123, Red Cloud's actions saved many lives.

One of the men he saved was Kenneth Bradshaws. Bradshaws, Red Cloud, and two other soldiers in the company were buddies who called themselves the Wild Bunch. Not long ago, Bradshaws recalled Red Cloud's bravery. "Hundreds died that day," he said. "If it were not for the alarm sounded by Mitchell Red Cloud, I would not be here today. This man, 'the Chief,' was a true warrior . . . and I owe him my life."

On April 3, 1951, Mitchell Red Cloud Jr. was awarded the Congressional Medal of Honor in a special ceremony at the Pentagon in Washington, D.C. His medal was given to his mother, Nellie, by General Omar Bradley. The citation that accompanied his medal read, in part, "Corporal Red Cloud's

United States soldiers shield themselves from exploding mortar shells. Mitchell Red Cloud's division as well the rest of the United Nations forces was forced to retreat in the early months of 1951.

dauntless courage and gallant self-sacrifice reflects the highest credit upon himself and upholds the esteemed traditions of the U.S. Army."[9]

In March 1955, Red Cloud's body was returned to the mission near his home. He was buried there on March 26. Since then, the Ho-Chunk ceremonial grounds where he is buried have been named in his honor. In 1967, his grave was marked with a special stone in his honor. Carved on that stone are words chosen to describe Red Cloud: "A son of a Winnebago chief and warriors who believe that when a man goes into battle, he expects to kill or be killed and if he dies, he will live forever."[10] In November 1983, Mitchell Red Cloud, Jr. was elected to the National Indian Hall of Fame.

Hiroshi Miyamura

8

Hiroshi Miyamura

Korean War Hero

On the night of April 24, 1951, U.S. Army Corporal Hiroshi Miyamura crouched in a deep trench in the hills near the village of Taejon-ni in North Korea. Miyamura was the leader of a machine gun squad in Company H of the 7th Infantry Regiment. For weeks the soldiers of the 7th had fought one battle after another against communist Chinese troops. Now, Miyamura and the men in his squad were part of a defensive force. They were protecting other troops that were pulling back after a fierce battle with enemy forces.

Earlier that night, twenty-six-year-old Miyamura had armed himself with two boxes of grenades, ammunition belts for his machine gun, and other weapons. He knew he and his men were likely to see action that night.[1] At about midnight, a bright white flare rose in the sky over the American position. The enemy was attacking.

"They didn't sneak up on us," Miyamura said in 1996. "They raised all kinds of hell, they blew whistles and bugles, they banged metal pots together, they made as much noise as they could . . . to scare us."[2]

In seconds, the defensive position occupied by Company H was swarming with screaming, shooting Red Chinese soldiers. Miyamura, called Hershey by his comrades, leaped from the trench and joined the battle. For the next several hours, he fought like a wild man. His bravery in that battle enabled most of the other men in his squad to escape. For his actions that night, he was ultimately awarded the Congressional Medal of Honor.

Miyamura was born in Gallup, New Mexico, on October 6, 1925. His father, Yaichi, and mother, Tori, came to America from Japan around 1910. First, they settled in a mining town not far from Gallup. In 1918, the Miyamuras moved to Gallup, where Yaichi opened a restaurant. Hiroshi was the fourth of six children; he had one brother and four sisters.

As a boy, Hiroshi attended school in Gallup. His sixth-grade teacher, unable to pronounce his given name, started calling him Hershey.[3] That nickname has stuck with him ever since. While he was growing up, Hershey enjoyed fishing with his uncle, who also lived in Gallup, and bowling. In addition, he loved boxing and fought in matches in and around Gallup.

Following his graduation from high school in 1943, Miyamura worked for a time as an auto mechanic in a garage owned by his uncle. At that time, the United States was in the throes of World War II. In 1945, he was drafted and assigned to the famed 442nd Regimental Combat Team. This U.S. Army Regiment, comprised entirely of Japanese Americans, was the most decorated regiment of the Second World War. Following his training, he was ordered to join the 442nd in Italy. "We were five days from Naples [Italy] on a troop ship when the war ended," Miyamura said. "So I didn't get to see any action in World War II."[4]

While he did not see action, he did join the 442nd in Italy and later returned as part of the famous outfit when it was honored with a huge ticker tape parade in New York City. "We were reviewed by President Truman," Miyamura said. "It was really something to be honored that way."[5]

At the end of World War II, Miyamura enlisted in the U.S. Army Reserve and returned to Gallup. He met Tsuruko (Terry), the young woman who was to become his wife, and worked in a local garage. After about a year, he moved to Milwaukee to attend a trade school. Then, in 1948, he came home on vacation. While at home, he was offered a job in an auto garage owned by his cousin. He accepted the job offer. In June of 1949, he and Terry were married.

As Hiroshi and Terry Miyamura began their married life, the United States was on the brink of the Korean Conflict. In June of 1950, a year after their marriage, the war began in earnest when eighty thousand North Korean troops invaded the South. In September of that same year, as the Chinese, aided by Russia, prepared to send an invasion force of about two hundred thousand troops across the Yalu River, Hiroshi Miyamura was recalled to active duty. By November, at about the time Mitchell Red Cloud was involved in his heroic action, Miyamura arrived in Korea.

When Miyamura arrived in Korea, U.N. forces, mostly American, were being driven far to the south by the enemy. Within weeks of his arrival, though, the 7th Infantry and other U.N. forces were again making their way north. As part of an operation the front line soldiers called the Meat Grinder, they pushed the communist Chinese and North Korean forces back across the dividing line between North and South Korea. Then, in late April 1951, the communist forces, now numbering more than 450,000 soldiers from North Korea and communist China, swooped across the 38th parallel and began hammering U.N. forces. All Miyamura and the other men of the 7th Infantry could do was withdraw and take defensive positions.

As the screaming, shooting Chinese soldiers overran his position, Hiroshi Miyamura jumped from the trench. Armed with his bayonet, he fought for his life. Witnesses said he killed at least ten enemy soldiers in hand-to-hand combat. He then returned to his position, where he administered first aid to his wounded comrades and had them carried to the rear.

Soon, another wave of Chinese soldiers attacked Miyamura and the remaining members of his squad. He fired his machine gun until all his ammunition was gone and then ordered the men close to him to withdraw. After disabling the gun so the enemy couldn't use it, he used his bayonet to fight his way to his squad's second machine gun. "I knew we were surrounded," he said. "I could see enemy soldiers behind us, all around us." Again he ordered the men near him to pull back while he stayed to provide covering fire. "All I could do was point the way for them to go and hope they could make it," he said.[6]

Miyamura stayed with the second gun until it jammed, killing as many as fifty of the enemy. According to the citation that accompanied his Medal of Honor, he was last seen by his troops, "fighting ferociously against an overwhelming number of enemy soldiers."[7]

For a time, his comrades who survived that night must have thought he'd been killed by the enemy. Instead, Miyamura used a grenade to destroy the machine gun and tried to make his own way to safety. He was running along a narrow gully when he suddenly came face-to-face with a Chinese soldier. "I bayoneted him, but fell backwards," he remembered. "As I fell, he threw a grenade at me. I kicked it back at him and it exploded, killing him. But when it exploded I was wounded by shrapnel. I was so scared I didn't even know I was wounded."[8]

Struggling to his feet, he ran on, hoping to find friendly forces. Instead, he tumbled into barbed wire strung by U.S. troops. His hands and legs were torn by the wire, but he freed himself and ran on. "Then I just couldn't go on anymore," he said.[9] He hid in a narrow gully. As the sun rose, he was discovered by Chinese troops, who took him prisoner.

For more than two years, Miyamura was held in captivity in a camp in the north. For the first year of his captivity, his wife and family had no idea he was alive. "After about a year we were allowed to write home," he said. "Of course we couldn't write the truth, we had to write what they told us to write." In the camp, he added, a lack of medical attention and starvation killed many prisoners. "I've seen a lot of young men die," he said.[10]

During most of Miyamura's time in the prison camp, the shooting war between the North Koreans and the U.N. forces was over. In fact, negotiations to end the war began about a month after his capture. It was late July of 1953, however, before a formal truce agreement ended the war.

On August 20 of that year, Miyamura walked into Freedom Village in Panmunjon, South Korea,

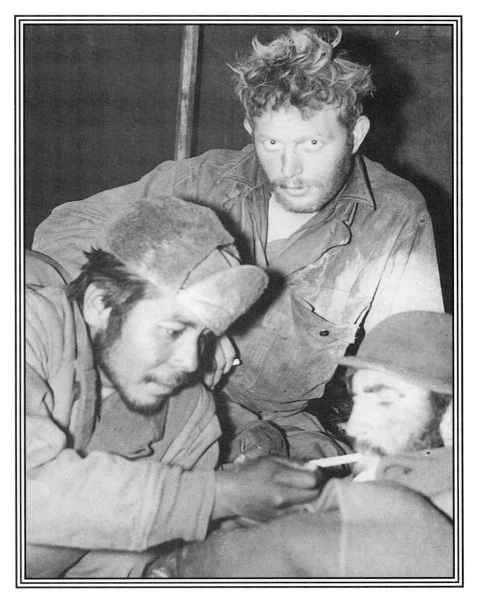

Three Americans rest after being released from a Chinese POW (Prisoner of War) camp. Hiroshi Miyamura was among the prisoners released after a truce was signed to stop the fighting in July of 1953.

Hiroshi Miyamura at a gathering of veterans. Miyamura often visits schools, teaching children about his war experiences.

where American POWs were released. After taking a shower and eating a bowl of ice cream, he was resting on a cot, he said, when a soldier told him a newsman wanted to talk to him.

"I walked into a room that was filled with lights. All I could see was a general standing at a table," he said. That general was Brigadier General Ralph Osborne, who was in charge of repatriation. As Miyamura stood at attention in his pajamas, General Osborne told him he'd been awarded his nation's highest military honor for his actions two years earlier. News of the award had been kept secret to protect Miyamura while he was in captivity. When he heard the news, Miyamura said, all he could think to say was, "What?"[11]

About three weeks later, Miyamura returned to Gallup. On the night of September 9, he and Terry danced together at a party in the hero's honor. Then they cut a red, white, and blue cake with the words, "Welcome Home, Hershey . . . For Valor Exceeding the Call of Duty . . . We Congratulate You" iced across its top.[12]

In 1996, Hershey Miyamura, age seventy-one, was living in Gallup with his wife, Terry. Retired, he frequently visited local schools to speak about his war experiences. "It's important that young people know about the contributions that have been made by Japanese Americans," he said. "Not by me, but by all the Japanese Americans."[13]

Jay Vargas

9

Jay Vargas

The Battle of Dai Do

In the spring of 1968 a fierce battle was waged near the tiny village of Dai Do in what was then known as the Republic of South Vietnam. On one side in this battle were U.S. Army and Marine Corps troops. On the other side were soldiers of the North Vietnamese Army (NVA). In the course of this battle, twenty-seven-year-old Marine Captain Jay Vargas fought with "conspicuous gallantry and intrepidity" as he put his own life at risk to save the lives of several of his comrades.[1] For his bravery, Captain Vargas earned his nation's highest military honor, the Medal of Honor.

Vargas was born on July 27, 1937, in Winslow, Arizona. He is the son of an Italian mother and

Spanish father who came to this country in 1917. His father was a newspaperman; his mother owned a store that sold western wear. He had three older brothers, Angelo, Frank, and Joseph.

Jay went to public schools in Winslow. As a boy, he loved sports and won a baseball scholarship to Arizona State University. He graduated with a degree in education in 1961.

As boys, Jay and his brothers were taught that the price of freedom is sacrifice and that hard work is the cost of success. Because of their early teaching, all four of the Vargas boys enlisted in the military. Angelo and Frank saw combat in World War II. Joseph fought in Korea. In May 1964, Jay enlisted in the U.S. Marines.[2]

By that time, the United States was already at war in Vietnam, in Southeast Asia. The story of this country's involvement in that war is long and complicated. At first, the U.S. supported the French as they fought Vietnamese communists who wanted to take control of the country. Later, after the French were defeated and Vietnam became a divided nation, America tried to help the people of South Vietnam when they were invaded by communist forces from the north. For a time, the U.S. sent soldiers to act as advisors to the Army of the Republic of Vietnam (ARVN). Then, in 1964, America entered the war as a combatant.

For several years, America fought battle after battle against the NVA and guerrilla forces. The war reached a major turning point in 1968. In January of that year, during the Vietnamese holiday of Tet, the communists attacked U.S. bases throughout the country. At that time, about three hundred thousand communist troops sneaked south across the Demilitarized Zone (DMZ), the dividing line between North and South Vietnam. Though the communists lost an estimated forty thousand soldiers in those attacks, they proved they could move a major force into South Vietnam and attack almost anywhere they wished.

Not long before the Tet offensive, Captain Jay Vargas arrived in Vietnam. He had joined the Marines in 1964 and had already seen one tour of combat in that country. Now he was back for a second tour.

On April 27, just four months after Tet, the NVA launched a large attack south of the DMZ. As the enemy moved south, they found themselves locked in battle with a Marine rifle company. In that battle, the commander of G Company, 2nd Battalion, 4th Marines, was wounded and had to be replaced. Vargas took his place.

It wasn't the first time Vargas was commander of G, or Golf Company. He had led Golf during the Tet Offensive but was replaced after he was twice wounded in action. Now he was back at the helm. The men in the company were happy to see him again. He had proven himself to be a good leader before, and his personality made him popular with

The first U.S. Marines land at Da Nang in South Vietnam in March, 1965. Vargas was serving his second tour in Vietnam when the Tet Offensive was launched by the North Vietnamese Army in January of 1968.

his men. "Everybody loves him," one who served with him later said.[3]

On the afternoon of April 30, three days after the initial contact between the Marines and NVA soldiers, Vargas and his men were in a clearing near the village of Lam Xuam, not far from Dai Do. At about 4 P.M., Vargas got orders to move his men to a staging area closer to Dai Do, where they were to join with other marines and prepare to attack the enemy. Within minutes, two large helicopters landed in the clearing. These choppers were supposed to carry Vargas and his men to the staging area.

Suddenly, the men and the helicopters in the clearing were under an intense attack. The choppers rose into the air and moved to safety. Vargas turned to one of his men. "No free ride today," he said. "We have to walk back."[4] For the next three hours, Vargas led the men in his company through about two miles of rice fields to the staging area. During that time, the enemy fired hundreds of artillery and mortar shells at the marines. "The troops were on the verge of panic," one of Vargas's men later said, "but Captain Vargas kept good control of the situation."[5]

During that march through the fields, Vargas was wounded by shell fragments. Still, he pressed on. At the staging area, he had a medic remove the shell fragments from his right leg. He found a pair of trousers that weren't torn and put them on to hide his wounds. He told the medic not to tell anybody that he was hurt. He wanted to continue leading his men.[6]

At the staging area, the men of G Company stretched out on the ground to rest. They knew the next morning they'd be in action. That night, Vargas hardly slept as he made sure all was ready for the coming attack on the village. "I remember closing my eyes for maybe thirty minutes," he later said.[7]

At about ten thirty the next morning, the men under Vargas's command attacked. They rushed across about seven hundred yards of open rice paddy as round after round of mortar, rocket, and artillery fire crashed around them. The men were finally able to reach the outskirts of the village. There, though, the NVA pinned them down. Captain Vargas then led his reserve troops to the aid of the trapped marines. As he edged toward a group of enemy machine-gun bunkers, grenade fragments tore into his right arm. Still, he fought on. He and one of his men attacked several bunkers and killed eight enemy soldiers inside them.

At first, it looked as if Vargas and his men would win the fight. Suddenly, however, the NVA launched a counterattack. Vargas ordered his men to take defensive positions near the edge of the village. Wave after wave of attackers was forced back. Golf held its position, but at day's end it was cut off from other marines in the area. And the fighting had been costly. More than half the approximately one hundred men who started the attack had been wounded or killed in the battle.

Throughout the night that followed, the enemy continued probing the company's position. Vargas called for artillery and air strikes all around his men. The strategy worked; the NVA was unable to overrun the marine position.

Early on the morning of May 2, marines of E Company joined Vargas and his men. Together, these companies tried again to clear Dai Do of enemy forces. During the day, the battle raged on. In midafternoon, the NVA launched a massive attack. Hundreds of enemy soldiers poured into Dai Do. According to a witness, "a fierce and brutal hand-to-hand battle ensued."[8] Vargas rallied his tired men and directed an orderly withdrawal back to the edge of Dai Do. In the fighting, Vargas was again wounded. Though this was his third wound in as many days, he again refused to leave the battlefield.

In this battle, the officer in charge of the battalion that included Golf was seriously wounded. Ignoring his own wounds, Vargas carried him to safety. He then returned to the fight to lead his men. As the men of G Company took a defensive position, he turned his attention to the wounded still in Dai Do. Time and again, he fought his way into the village to save wounded men. According to witnesses, Vargas saved at least seven men by his actions on this day.[9]

Finally, late in the day, more marines arrived on the scene. A strong defensive perimeter was established.

Vargas currently works for the state government in California, as secretary of the Deparment of Veterans Affairs.

Slowly, the fighting stopped. The night was quiet as the NVA slipped away into the rice paddies and jungle around the village. The cost to the men of G Company had been tremendous. Of the one hundred men who had started the attack on the morning of May 1, only about thirty-six were not killed or wounded in the battle.

On May 3, Vargas was flown from the battle site in a medevac helicopter. After recuperating, he returned to active duty. He remained in the Marine Corps after the war and was ultimately made a regimental commander. He retired as a colonel. On May 14, 1970, just shy of two years after the battle of Dai Do, Vargas, then a major, was awarded the Medal of Honor by President Richard Nixon in a ceremony at the White House.

Vargas is currently the secretary of the California Department of Veterans Affairs. He recently said he felt "proud and humbled" when he was awarded the Medal of Honor. While in the Marines, he also received the Silver Star, Navy Commendation, five Purple Hearts, and the Republic of Vietnam Cross of Gallantry. Vargas and his wife, Dottie, have three grown daughters, Kris, Julie, and Gina.

Randall Shughart

10

Gary Gordon and Randall Shughart

Valor in Somalia

It was an October afternoon in 1993. A flight of helicopters rose into the sky over the African nation of Somalia. On board the choppers were U.S. Army Rangers. With the rangers were members of a group known as Delta Force. These were soldiers trained to stop terrorists. Their orders were to surround a house in the city of Mogadishu. There they were to capture a rebel leader named Mohamed Farah Aidid. This man and his followers were waging war on U.N. forces in Somalia.

Soon the choppers were in the air over the house. As the whirlybirds hovered, American troops slid down ropes that dangled to the ground below. Guns at the ready, they attacked and quickly captured twenty-four of Aidid's men. Suddenly, Aidid's troops on the ground raked the choppers in the air with shoulder-launched rockets and fire from automatic weapons. Two choppers that were giving air support to the troops on the ground were hit, and they crashed.

As soon as the two choppers were shot down, American troops swung into action. Army rangers were quickly able to surround and offer some help to the men of one of the downed helicopters. However, the second chopper was surrounded by Aidid's forces. Ground forces could not reach it.

A helicopter with Sergeant First Class Randall Shughart and Master Sergeant Gary Gordon on board was sent to offer help to the crew of the wrecked chopper. Heavy fire from the ground made it impossible for their helicopter to remain over the wrecked craft. Shughart and Gordon immediately volunteered to jump into the firefight. At first, they were ordered not to go. They volunteered again. Again they were told to stay put. The two men volunteered yet again. This time, they were given the go-ahead by the chopper pilot.[1]

When the helicopter carrying the two soldiers tried to get close to the crash site, it was almost shot out of the sky. Fire from automatic rifles and grenade launchers raked the craft. Retreating for a moment, the chopper finally was able to hover near the ground about one hundred yards from the men they were trying to help. The two soldiers slid down ropes from their hovering craft to the ground below. In the hours that followed, Gary Gordon and Randall Shughart fought, and died, to save their fellow soldiers. For their bravery on that day, each was awarded the Congressional Medal of Honor.

The fierce battle in Mogadishu had its real beginning about five years earlier. At that time, Somalia, a tiny nation on the east central coast of Africa, was torn by civil war. As a result of this civil war the nation's economy was disrupted. Crops failed, and millions of people faced starvation.

While the country was devastated and thousands of Somalian people died, the world took little notice. Then, thanks to news reports, particularly televised reports showing innocent women and children dying in refugee camps, the world demanded action on the part of authorities. In mid-1992, the United Nations mounted a relief effort. It tried to provide food and other aid to the suffering citizens of Somalia. These relief efforts failed, as warring clans stole food and other supplies meant for the starving.

In late 1992, American soldiers were sent to Somalia. Their job was to see to it that aid reached the needy. Along with other U.N. forces, they were also ordered to disarm clan forces. This meant they had to take weapons away from the followers of Aidid, the most powerful of all clan leaders. Aidid vowed not to give up his weapons and to resist any efforts to make him disarm. He was as good as his word. On June 5, 1993, his forces attacked and killed twenty-five U.N. troops. As a result of that attack, the focus of the U.N. forces shifted from feeding people to capturing Aidid. For several months, he was an elusive target. Then, on October 3, 1993, the Americans got word that the rebel leader was meeting with some of his supporters in a building in southeast Mogadishu. A force, including Sergeants Shughart and Gordon, was sent to capture the rebel.

Randall Shughart was born on August 13, 1958, in Lincoln, Nebraska. He and his family moved to Pennsylvania not long after his birth. As a boy, growing up on Wildwood Lane in the Central Pennsylvania town of Newville, he enjoyed the outdoors. He and a friend, Neal McCulloch, hung out together. They hunted in the rural countryside, flew kites together, and played "pickup" football games on Sunday afternoons. "Randy loved the outdoors," McCulloch remembered. "It gave him a respect for life."[2]

Shughart joined the army in 1976, immediately after he graduated from high school. After his first enlistment, he tried civilian life for about a year, but then went back into the army. By all accounts, he loved being a soldier.

"God gave him a special gift," McCulloch said. "He let him know what he was meant to be, a professional soldier."[3]

Gary Gordon was thirty-three years old when he fought at Shughart's side in the battle on the street of Mogadishu. He was born in Lincoln, Maine, on August 30, 1960. As a boy, growing up in New

England, he was called Bugsy because of his front teeth, which stuck out when he grinned. He loved to draw and sketch. His favorite subjects were soldiers, guns, and tanks. He played running back on his high school football team. Though Gary was small for a football player at 5 feet 8 inches and about 150 pounds, he was "a human battering ram," his cousin and boyhood friend Roger Stevens said. He also found time to read books about spies and soldiers. When he was eleven years old, he visited the public library in his hometown and checked out a small book about the Medal of Honor.[4]

Like his partner, Shughart, Gordon enlisted in the army soon after his graduation from high school. He left home on Valentine's Day in 1979. Within a year, he qualified for the Army's Special Forces, the Green Berets. Then, in the late 1980s, he became a member of the elite Delta Force. He was sent to Somalia in August of 1993.

On the ground in Mogadishu, Shughart and Gordon, armed with sniper rifles and pistols, battled their way through a maze of shacks and tumbledown houses to the men they wanted to help. As soon as they reached the downed helicopter, they pulled its crewmen to safety. They then took up positions from which they could fire at the enemy and keep them at bay. Shughart patrolled the perimeter he and Gordon established, killing an unknown number of enemy fighters. When his ammunition ran out, he was shot and killed by some of Aidid's men.[5]

99

Gary Gordon

Gordon also fired until he was out of ammo. He then ran back to the downed helicopter and recovered some weapons and more ammunition. He gave the downed pilot some of his own ammunition, even though that left him short. He also used the radio to call for help. After returning to the perimeter and using all but a few rounds of ammo, he returned to the downed helicopter yet again. There he found only a rifle with five rounds of ammunition. He gave the weapon to the pilot. "Good luck," he said, and then ran back to the perimeter armed only with his pistol. He continued fighting until he was shot and killed.[6]

Chief Warrant Officer Michael Durant, the pilot saved by Gordon and his partner, was captured and later freed. While in captivity, though, he was humiliated by Aidid's men. He was tortured and dragged through the streets of Mogadishu. When he returned to America in late 1994, he gave credit to Shughart and Gordon for saving his life. "Without a doubt," he said, "I owe my life to these two men and their bravery."[7]

In a ceremony in the East Room of the White House in 1994, President William Clinton praised the two medal winners. "Gary Gordon and Randall Shughart died in the most courageous and selfless way any human being can act," he said. "They risked their lives without hesitation. They gave their lives to save others."

The President went on to quote words of the prophet Isaiah, words that are etched in stone on the wall of the Special Forces Memorial Court at Fort Bragg, Kentucky: "I heard the voice of the Lord saying, 'Whom shall I send, and who will go for us?'"

"Master Sergeant Gary Gordon and Sergeant First Class Randall Shughart answered that call," President Clinton said.[8]

Shughart left behind his wife, Stephanie. Gary Gordon was survived by his wife, Carmen, and two small children.

Chapter Notes

Chapter 1

1. Charles O'Neill, *Wild Train* (New York: Random House, 1956), p. 63.

2. Craig Angle, *The Great Locomotive Chase* (Rouzerville, Pa.: self-published, 1992), p. 29.

3. Ibid., p. 29.

4. O'Neill, p. 81.

5. Angle, p. 163.

6. O'Neill, p. 166.

7. Ibid., p. 191.

8. Ibid., pp. 348, 349.

9. Ibid., p. 349.

Chapter 2

1. Luis F. Emilio, *A Brave Black Regiment* (Salem, N.H.: Ayer Company, 1990), p. 81.

2. Ruford Logan and Michael Winston, eds., *Dictionary of American Negro Biography* (New York: W. W. Norton, 1982), p. 90.

3. Jack Fincher, "The Hard Fight was Getting into the Fight At All," *Smithsonian*, October 1990, p. 46.

4. Logan and Winston, p. 90.

5. Emilio, p. 76.

6. Ibid., p. 79.

7. Ibid., p. 80.

8. Logan and Winston, p. 91.

Chapter 3

1. Medal of Honor Citation, dated November 11, 1865, signed by President Andrew Johnson.

2. Charles Snyder, *Dr. Mary Walker, The Little Lady in Pants,* reprint edition (New York: Arno Press, 1974), p. 13.

3. Ibid.

4. *Minneapolis Tribune,* July 4, 1897, p. 1.

5. Snyder, p. 18.

6. Elizabeth Leonard, *Yankee Women* (New York: W. W. Norton, 1994), p. 129.

7. Snyder, p. 41.

8. A. Wilder, *History of Medicine. A Brief Outline of Medical History and Sects of Physicians from the Earliest Historic Period* (New Sharon, Maine: New England Eclectic Publishing Co., 1901), p. 571. Cited by Allen Spiegel, "Mary Edwards Walker, MD: The Only Woman Ever Awarded the Congressional Medal of Honor," *New York State Journal of Medicine,* July 1991, p. 298.

9. Snyder, p. 46.

10. Dumas Malone, ed., *Dictionary of American Biography* (New York: Charles Scribner's Sons, 1936), p. 352.

11. Mary Binker, "Feminism's Tinker, Tailor, Physician, Spy," *Insight on the News,* July 24, 1995, p. 27.

12. Leonard, p. 156.

13. Allen Spiegel, "Mary Edwards Walker, MD: The Only Woman Ever Awarded the Congressional Medal of Honor," *New York State Journal of Medicine,* July 1991, p. 297.

Chapter 4

1. Edward V. Rickenbacker, *Rickenbacker, An Autobiography* (Englewood Cliffs, N.J.: Prentice Hall, 1967), p. 105.

2. Ezra Bowen, ed., *Knights of the Air*, 2nd ed. (Alexandria, VA: Time-Life Books, 1981), p. 153.

3. Rickenbacker, p. 20.

4. Ibid., p. 28.

5. Kenneth Jackson, ed., *Dictionary of American Biography, Supplement Nine* (New York: Charles Scribner's Sons, 1994), p. 657.

6. Rickenbacker, pp. 74–75.

7. Ibid., p. 110.

8. Ibid., p. 126.

9. Ibid., p. 258.

Chapter 5

1. Brian McGinty, "Alvin York: Soldier of the Lord," *American History Illustrated,* November 1986, p. 40.

2. Ibid.

3. David D. Lee, *Sergeant York, an American Hero* (Lexington: University Press of Kentucky, 1985), p. 18.

4. McGinty, p. 40.

5. Lee, p. 19.

6. McGinty, p. 40.

7. Lee, p. 22.

8. Alvin C. York, "Sergeant York's Own Story: A Lecture," quoted in Lee, p. 26.

9. Ibid.

10. Don Lawson, *The United States in World War I* (New York: Abelard-Schuman, 1963), pp. 134–136.

11. Lee, p. 36.

12. Lawson, p. 133.

Chapter 6

1. W. L. White, *They Were Expendable* (New York: Harcourt, Brace, 1942), p. 70.

2. William B. Breuer, *Sea Wolf: A Biography of John D. Bulkeley* (Novato, Calif.: Presidio Press, 1989), p. 5.

3. White, p. 5.

4. Breuer, p. 25.

5. *New York Daily News*, January 21, 1942, p. 1.

6. Breuer, p. 54.

7. Ibid., p. 64.

8. Richard Pearson, "John Bulkeley Dies at 84; Vice Admiral, WWII Hero," *Washington Post*, April 8, 1996, p. B6.

Chapter 7

1. "Memories of Corporal Mitchell Red Cloud, Jr.," speech given by Kenneth Bradshaws, reprinted in the *Ho-chunk Wo-lduk* tribal newspaper, July 1994, p. 3.

2. Ibid.

3. Toddy Porath, "Looking Back Jackson County," *Black River Falls Banner-Journal*, July 10, 1991, p. 7B.

4. "War Hero's Marker to be Dedicated," *Black River Falls Banner-Journal*, September, 1967, p. 10.

5. "Looking Back Jackson County."

6. Ibid.

7. Statement of Captain Walter Conway, *Congressional Record*, April 4, 1951, p. 3,248.

8. Medal of Honor Citation, General Order No. 26, April 1951.

9. Ibid.

10. "Looking Back Jackson County."

Chapter 8

1. Author interview with Hiroshi Miyamura, October 24, 1996.

2. Ibid.

3. Ibid.

4. Ibid.

5. Ibid.

6. Ibid.

7. Medal of Honor Citation, General Order No. 85, November 4, 1953.

8. Author interview.

9. Ibid.

10. Ibid.

11. Ibid.

12. "Hershey Is Honored at JACL Party Here," *Gallup Independent,* vol. 64, no. 205, September 10, 1953, p. 1f.

13. Author interview.

Chapter 9

1. Medal of Honor Citation of Captain Jay Vargas, presented May 14, 1970.

2. Author interview with Jay Vargas, 1996.

3. Keith Nolan, *The Magnificent Bastards* (New York: Dell, 1994), p. 22.

4. Ibid., p. 92.

5. Ibid.

6. Ibid., p. 94.

7. Ibid., p. 96.

8. Official Document submitted to Congress and the President of the United States, undated, supplied by Congressional Medal of Honor Society, Mt. Pleasant, South Carolina, p. 3.

9. Ibid.

Chapter 10

1. Remarks at the Presentation Ceremony for the Congressional Medal of Honor, Transcript, Superintendent of Documents, May 23, 1994, p. 1.

2. Wendy Lippert, "Somalian Conflict Claims the Life of Big Spring Graduate," *The Valley Times-Star*, Newville, Pa., vol. 134, no. 41, p. 1.

3. Ibid.

4. Cindy Anderson, "Leaving Lincoln," *Yankee Magazine*, November 1995, vol. 59, no. 11, p. 58.

5. Medal of Honor Citation, Randall Shughart, provided by Congressional Medal of Honor Society, Mt. Pleasant, S.C.

6. Medal of Honor Citation, Gary Gordon, provided by Congressional Medal of Honor Society, Mt. Pleasant, S.C.

7. Remarks at presentation ceremony, p. 2.

8. Ibid.

Further Reading

Angle, W. Craig. *The Great Locomotive Chase: More on the Andrews Raid & the First Medal of Honor.* Rouzerville, PA: Angle, W. C., 1992.

Carroll, John. *Medal of Honor: History & Recipients.* Mattituck, N.Y.: Amereon, Limited, 1976.

DeLong, Kent. *War Heroes: Stories of Congressional Medal of Honor Recipients.* Westport, CT: Greenwood Publishing Group, Inc., 1993.

Fremon, David K. *Japanese-American Internment in American History.* Springfield, N.J.: Enslow Publishers, Inc., 1996.

Jordan, Kenneth N., Sr. *Yesterday's Heroes: 433 Men of World War II Awarded the Medal of Honor 1941–1945.* Atglen, PA: Schiffer Publishing, Limited, 1996.

———. *Heroes of Our Time: 239 Men of the Vietnam War Awarded the Medal of Honor 1964–1972.* Atglen, PA: Schiffer Publishing, Limited, 1995.

Kent, Deborah. *The Vietnam War: "What Are We Fighting For?"* Springfield, N.J.: Enslow Publishers, Inc., 1994.

Kent, Zachary. *The Civil War: "A House Divided."* Springfield, N.J.: Enslow Publishers, Inc., 1994.

Kent, Zachary. *World War I: "The War to End Wars."* Springfield, N.J.: Enslow Publishers, Inc., 1994.

Lang, George, Raymond L. Collins, and Gerard White. *Medal of Honor Recipients, 1863–1994.* New York: Facts on File, Inc., 1995.

Lemon, Peter C. *Beyond the Medal: A Journey from Their Hearts to Yours.* Golden, CO: Fulcrum Publishing, 1997.

Snyder, Charles M. *Dr. Mary Walker: The Little Lady in Pants.* North Stratford, N.H.: Ayer Company Publishers, Inc., 1977.

Stein, R. Conrad. *The Korean War: "The Forgotten War."* Springfield, N.J.: Enslow Publishers, Inc., 1994.

———. *World War II in Europe: "America Goes to War."* Springfield, N.J.: Enslow Publishers, Inc., 1994.

———. *World War II in the Pacific: "Remember Pearl Harbor."* Springfield, N.J.: Enslow Publishers, Inc., 1994.

Index